CONTENT MARKETING PRIMER

Developing your Content Strategy Roadmap

Dr Savi S Arora, PGDMS, MBA, PhD

Knowledge Hemispheres Limited

Find more Best Practice Management Guides at:
www.Savileaders.com
(Example is Leadership)

To my Family for all their support and encouragement...
Just write it!

Today there is an increasing tide of books focusing on Content Management, ranging from strategy development, user experience, design, and the study of web optimisation.

As we continue to sift through information overload and the resulting attention economy. Authentic storytelling will enhance your brand and sustain your customers' interest in your brand and product.

This primer purely focuses on Content marketing strategy formulation and imparting associated content management disciplines for the development of an effective associated roadmap.

Tools and Techniques are key ingredients to establish a foundation for success as you develop your online presence, either for internal or external projects

DR SAVI ARORA, PGDMS, MBA, PHD

CONTENTS

ACKNOWLEDGEMENT

My experience is based on delivering real world projects and consider that life is a journey, with an aim to learn and support others on route.

I'm appreciative to creative souls that continue to light the way to discover new pathways for project and personal success.

1 - INTRODUCTION

Creating a successful content marketing strategy requires a well-defined vision, a deep understanding of your audience and a competitive content strategy. Our primer provides an insight into all these areas.

Essentially, this book will guide you through the essential steps of developing your content strategy roadmap, including:

- **Defining Your Content Vision:**

  Your content vision is the foundation of your content strategy. It is a clear statement of what you want to achieve through your content and how you will differentiate yourself from your competitors. We will provide you with guidance on how to define your content vision and align it with your business goals.

- **Conducting Content Analysis:**

  Understanding your audience's needs, preferences, and behaviour is essential for creating effective content. This book will show you how to conduct a comprehensive and core content analysis to identify content gaps, opportunities, and trends.

- **Developing a Competitive Content Strategy:**

  A competitive content strategy is critical for standing out in a crowded marketplace. Examples will demonstrate how to develop a competitive content strategy that sets you apart from your competitors and resonates with your audience.

- **Implementing a Content Maturity Model:**

  A Content Maturity Model is a framework that helps you assess and improve your content marketing efforts. Guidance will be provided on how to use it to optimise your content strategy together with tips on governance.

- **Creating Customer-Valued Content:**

  Creating customer-valued content is the key to building trust, loyalty, and engagement with your audience. This book will provide advice on practical and creative examples that you can use to connect with your audience and achieve your content marketing goals.

  By the end of this book, you will have a solid understanding of how to develop through tools and techniques a content strategy roadmap that aligns with your business goals, resonates with your audience, and sets you apart from your competitors.

2 - DEVELOPING AN INSPIRING CONTENT MARKETING MISSION STATEMENT

Whether it's a podcast, article, blog, or website content outlining a product description, knowing your audience is key. Start off by thinking through if it's for a wider or niche address. Using basic critical thinking categories can help.

The Who What Why and When Questions:

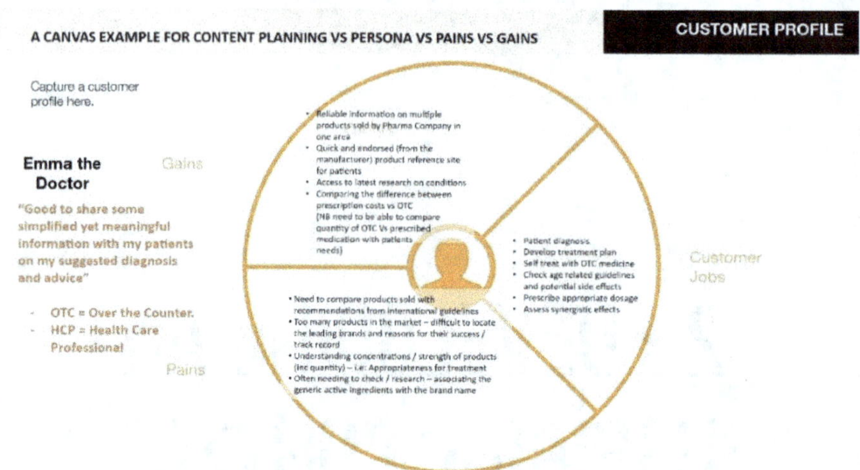

A CANVAS EXAMPLE FOR CONTENT PLANNING VS PERSONA VS PAINS VS GAINS
CUSTOMER PROFILE
Capture a customer profile here.
Emma the Doctor
"Good to share some simplified yet meaningful information with my patients on my suggested diagnosis and advice"
- OTC = Over the Counter.
- HCP = Health Care Professional
Gains
Pains
Customer Jobs
• Reliable information on multiple products sold by Pharma Company in one area
• Quick and endorsed (from the manufacturer) product reference site for patients
• Access to latest research on conditions
• Comparing the difference between prescription costs vs OTC (NB need to be able to compare quantity of OTC Vs prescribed medication with patients needs)
• Patient diagnosis
• Develop treatment plan
• Self treat with OTC medicine
• Check age related guidelines and potential side effects
• Prescribe appropriate dosage
• Assess synergistic effects
• Need to compare products sold with recommendations from international guidelines
• Too many products in the market – difficult to locate the leading brands and reasons for their success / track record
• Understanding concentrations / strength of products (inc quantity) – i.e: Appropriateness for treatment
• Often needing to check / research – associating the generic active ingredients with the brand name

Who:

Who refers to the target audience, for example: Buyers, Sellers, or Internal teams? It is key that if you're unable to understand what someone will gain from consuming your brand's content, your audience won't see a compelling reason to engage with it. Using a canvas to map the value of content for the intended audience is an ideal way to derive the true mission of your online presence.

What:

Combined with the latter, how will it support the recipients of your content?

Why:

Why is content an important ingredient of your marketing mix in the context of People, Price, Placement and Product description and will it support the promotion of your brand?

When:

How often will the content need to be updated or is its evergreen?

Writing a content mission statement can help you refine, agree, and set clear parameters for a successful content strategy, also known as framing the true purpose of your content. Successful agreement of your strategy will lead both your drive to be creative and strategic decision-making within the organisation. Everything else will follow for example, the ability to develop meaningful stories (storytelling) and the creation of compelling content to sustain your intended audience's attention.

The Attention Economy

We also need to consider that we are living in the 'attention economy'. The phrase "attention economy" was first coined by psychologist and economist Herbert A. Simon in 1971. He predicted that in an information-rich world, as people are bombarded with more and more information, it becomes increasingly difficult to capture and maintain their attention.

In 1997, Michael H. Goldhaber wrote that the global economy is shifting from a material-based economy to one based on the capacity of human attention. Many services online are offered for free. In the attention economy, attention is not only a resource but a currency: users pay for a service with their attention. The term attention economy refers to the range of economic activities based on people's attention being treated as a scarce and highly desirable resource to be captured and maintained.

Therefore, having an effective content management strategy means creating content that is valuable, relevant, and engaging. To be successful in the attention economy, content creators must focus on providing value to their audience, whether through informative articles, entertaining videos, or other types of content that resonate with their target market.

They must also be strategic in the distribution of their content to reach their intended audience in the places and at the times they are most likely to be receptive.

A strong content mission statement reflects your business values and helps you distinguish your storytelling from other content competing for your audience's attention.

It can also inform content decisions on the creative side, including categorising type of content for topic focus. This will lead to how stories will be formulated and published in terms of format and available platforms.

Content components working in harmony:

Ensuring that content assets, for example: Video, audio, text, and immersive tools (virtual reality) will create desirable experiences for the intended audience.

Consistency:

Rationalised or selective use of content assets, for example, if a dental nurse is featured in all the same content imagery or his/her fashion is not in vogue, without understanding the metadata associated with the image could lead to subtle outcomes such as off-brand or overuse of the same asset. This will result in unintended messaging.

Studying your company mission statement is a good place to start. If it is well formulated from the outset, it can be central to all the activities of an organisation.

A driver for why:

Deriving audience benefits can stem from the development of tested audience personas. This is when an organisation tries to uncover audience needs vs desires. A useful tool is the application of a canvas.

The Role of Audience Personas

Audience personas validate a customer's most pressing needs. Place yourself in the shoes of your client and ask why your business is suited to deliver on those audience needs and how your approach stands out from other brands your audience might also be exposed to. What value will your content give your audience over and above your nearest rival and if possible, the personal impact it may have. The latter is not something that is based solely on logic and data (based on analytics or market research data) since there's a strong emotional component involved.

Strategies for effective content development

Set goals - that are realistic and measurable. Stretch targets can also be established at this early stage. Consider aligning these goals with the organisation's marketing strategy and company mission statement.

Develop a good understanding of your customer journey - Harvard Business Review once outlined that sometimes in a firm there can be over twenty routes to connect with a company. Everything from consumers to service providers to escalations such as product returns. Often it is poor customer service that the customer remembers the most and can sway them to return if positive or be lost if the experience is poor. Consider also how customers are converted from prospect to potential and loyal customer.

Plan - via shared content calendars and collation of content is important. For example, does your podcast refer to other available content that is either exclusive to your or available through partnerships via other firms.

Maintain great writing - Style, Spelling, Tone, and Grammar are all part of a professional consistent content voice for your organisation.

Optimisation for good online pick-up aka resonation so that your audience would like to read or engage more - Although this book doesn't go into detail on how visuals/rich media and structure support how search engines index your content. Authenticity is important together with consistent and regular postings. Significant and relevant content to your subject matter will get you noticed online aka virtually.

Researching your target & Storytelling - Develop customer personas and test them on an ongoing basis. Combined with storytelling it's all about being positive with focus on value and staying genuine. The latter means ensuring consistency with your identity. Link to the meaning behind the brand.

Mapping Customer Needs using a Canvas & surveying before you start documenting.

Use a canvas for customer pain and gain mapping - This helps to identify your customers' gains and potential gains that your company can give them. Back up your lens with understanding and documenting what success looks like both internally and externally.

Ensure that your canvas is not based on assumptions. It's important to stay relevant and one way of doing this is that famous marketing activity known as research aka Market Research. Questions on any survey should not be leading or suggestive.

Although User Experience studies can involve Psychoanalysis, together with agree web behaviour analysis using hand and eye tracking to optimise navigation. The true test is if the original requirement for the product has 'legs!

Omnichannel in the context of content marketing

This refers to the strategy of creating and distributing marketing content across multiple channels, such as social media, email, blogs, podcasts, videos, and more, in a way that provides a seamless and consistent experience for the audience. The goal of an omnichannel approach is to make sure that the message, branding, and tone are consistent across all channels, and that the content is optimised for each specific platform, while also enabling customers to interact with the brand across channels and devices. This approach recognizes that customers engage with brands in different ways and at different times, and it seeks to provide a unified and integrated experience across all touchpoints, ultimately leading to higher customer engagement and loyalty.

Content can be repurposed, for example, develop once, use many times through different outlets / channels or forms. One approach is to build relationships with partners that reflect your brand, value, and complementary products. Another route to achieve exposure is through building disclaimer-based industry partnerships and links to academia.

Loop back to check your content strategy - This is achieved by agreeing analytic measures from the outset, for example, through monitoring and auditing your content.-

3 - CONTENT ANALYSIS

Content analysis is the process of analysing content to see how it's currently performing. You can conduct an analysis of your own brand to see how your current content marketing strategy is working. By doing this, you can see if you're meeting your content goals and if you need to make any improvements.

Borrowing from Clinical Analysis!

If we borrow from scientific research methodologies, an approach known as the - Clinical-qualitative content analysis technique, comprises seven steps:

1. Editing material for analysis.
2. Floating reading.
3. Construction of the units of analysis.
4. Construction of codes of meaning.
5. General refining of the codes and the Construction of categories.
6. Discussion.
7. Validity

In the same way, web-based content analysis helps you to analyse and understand how your competitors' content is performing. This will lead you to make more informed decisions about your content marketing campaigns. For instance, through a content analysis, you can see if there are any keywords your competitors rank for that you don't. You can then create new content around those keywords that help improve your website's organic traffic. Content analysis can help you measure effectiveness, for example: visitors, backlinks created, and where your content ranks on search engines. You can also focus on your conversion rates. The conversion rate measures the number of website visitors that complete a desired goal. This can include making a purchase, signing up for a newsletter, or downloading a white paper or eBook. This will help you see what content is most popular with your readers and if there are any blogs or articles that are currently lagging or subjects that you talk about that are trending. For example, you might notice that some of your articles or blogs are outperforming your videos. Armed with this knowledge you can increase the production of your written content to continue engaging with your customers.

Building a dashboard

There are many ways to slice and dice your vegetables!

A good way to analyse your content is to consider the original goals of the intended marketing campaign. Therefore, all metrics need to link directly to the desire of the latter. Typical factors to view are:

Sales:

Are they rising, falling, or staying static?

Remarketing:

Considered in the context of targeting users with ads based on their previous internet activity.

Search Ranking:

Check your current ranking, popular relevant and popular keywords used by competitors.

Multiple Visits to your Site:

Using a Customer Relationship Management (CRM) tool, you can track a visitor every time they visit your site via a tracking cookie in their browser. The cookie marks every page they visit on your site and when they leave and return. The cookie stays with the user's browser until they clear them. Lead scoring allows you to track your visitors' behaviour and determine their level of interest in your products or services based on what they do. After users interact with your social media or content, the CRM gives them a score based on their interests. You can then see the scores and focus your resources on customers who are most likely to make a purchase. Using CRM tracking and lead scoring, you can determine whether your content encourages users to visit your site multiple times and whether it produces high-value leads.

Customer Engagement Tools:

Tools are also available to see if a user keeps looking at the same product per visit. Tracking via separate consented tags can help to optimise the customer's experience. For example, if the customer/ visitor keeps looking at the same car and associated colours and options, if they've done this over their last 5 visits, on their 6th visit they will see what they last saw or was most popular to them.

Page Views and Unique Page Views:

Every time someone loads a page on your website—whether on mobile or a desktop—that page receives a page view. However, if a visitor to your website finds your site from Google, clicks to different pages, and then hits the "back" button until they leave the website again, every time they view a page, that counter goes up. Unique page tracking is available.

Time on Page:

This metric is useful because it gives you a powerful indicator of how much your website visitors like your content.

Engagement Metrics:

When people engage with your content, it's a sign that they feel connected to it and have become invested in what they're reading.

With these initial metrics you can quickly establish how much your site is resonating with your visitors and immediate corrective actions.

Once the dashboard is in place you can also progress trend analysis to develop more effective content that is also considerate of your immediate marketing needs.

How To perform a Competitive Content Marketing Analysis

Here is a list of steps to help you perform a competitive content marketing analysis:

List Your Major Competitors

When you compile a list of your major competitors, manage, and analyse the information more easily by using a spreadsheet. Add the names and domains of your top competitors. This includes your direct competitors and indirect competitors. Your direct competitors are any company that sells the same products or services that you do. For example, let's say your business sells fancy pens with refillable ink. A direct competitor might sell pens very similar to yours.

Indirect competitors are any company that sells products or services like yours, but not the same. Most often, your products and the competitor's products will each solve the same customer challenge. For instance, if you sell fancy pens with refillable ink, an indirect competitor might sell mechanical pencils with refillable graphite. It's not the same product, but they both meet similar consumer needs.

Find Their Target Audience

Your target audience and your competitors' target audiences should be relatively the same. One way to find their audience is by looking at their website's title tag and meta description.

If your competitor is an e-commerce website, a Google search might also list some of its most popular pages or products.

Seeing your competitor's top product and service pages can help you discover what copy and content produce the most traffic. Consider and learn from the format of those pages and how each company defines its products. Does the company style its pages in a way to target a specific audience? How does it describe its products or services in a way that's engaging to its customers? By reviewing your competitors' websites, you can have a better understanding of how to attract your target audience and improve your company's site and content.

Analyse Their SEO Metrics

There are many metrics that make up a business' Search Engine Optimisation (SEO), including organic traffic numbers, top-performing keywords, top-performing pages, and backlinks.

When comparing this information to your own website, you can find areas to improve and find potential gaps in your content strategy. Gaps in the strategy include keywords you're not ranking for and domains that might syndicate your content.

Review Their Content

Looking over your competitors' content is a great way to see what they're producing and what their audiences are interacting with. Browse their websites and see what type of content they're creating.

Some content to look out for includes:

- Blogs
- Augmented Reality simulations for product placement
- Research articles
- Podcasts
- Webinars
- White papers and eBooks
- Videos
- Online Courses

On your spreadsheet, note how much content they generate for each category and how often they post. This can help you better understand the content marketing schedule and size of their marketing team. How many viewers share their content, comment on it, or like it?

Make Comparisons

Take your list of content for each competitor and compare all of them. See if each company follows a similar content strategy. For instance, do most companies focus on creating blogs versus video content? If so, are those companies more successful or less successful compared to the others? Do they use Influencers and how are they (the influencers) using social media to draw attention to your product or brand?

4 - CONTENT MARKETING STRATEGY PRINCIPLES

The definition of content marketing is the process of publishing written and visual material online with the purpose of attracting more leads for your business. These can include blog posts, pages, eBooks, infographics, videos, and more. Content must be purposeful, authentic, and targeted for the right audience.

Outbound Vs Inbound marketing strategies

However, content marketing is more about purposefully tailoring your pages, videos, eBooks, and posts to your target audience so that they find you the inbound way rather than the outbound way. Today, outbound marketing strategies (or anything that interrupts your audience members) aren't as effective at resonating with and converting audience members as they once were.

Today, your content needs to reach your audience in a way that feels natural. A common way of doing this is by creating a narrative for your content — or telling a story. In doing so, your content will feel more authentic, engaging, and tailored to your audience. There are many types of content marketing that you may choose to incorporate in your strategy — here are some of the most common:

Online Content Marketing

Online content marketing refers to any material you publish online, but more specifically, it refers to your web pages. A strong online content marketing strategy will help you rank higher in the search engine results pages (SERPs) and get you in front of the right people at the right time.

Social Media Content Marketing

With over 4.2 billion global social media users, it's easy to understand why so many businesses invest in social media marketing. There are several platforms (e.g., Facebook, Instagram, Pinterest, LinkedIn,

Snapchat) to work with and several ways you can create and share content on each of them (e.g. photos, live videos, pre-recorded videos, stories).

Infographic Content Marketing

Infographics display content, information, and data in an easy-to-understand, graphic format. With a mix of simple wording, short statements, and clear images, infographics are a great way to effectively communicate your content. They work well if you're trying to distil an educational and/ or complex topic down so all audience members can understand it.

Blog Content Marketing

Blogs are a powerful type of inbound content and allow for a lot of creativity in terms of their purpose and topic. With a blog, you can do things like promote other internal and external content and blog articles via links, add social share buttons, and incorporate product information.

Podcast Content Marketing

More than 60 million people listen to podcasts across the Spotify and Apple Podcasts platforms. For this reason, many businesses and media outlets have begun creating and sharing their own podcasts.

Podcasts allow for a lot of creativity as they can be about any topic of choice. Additionally, you determine other factors related to the podcast such as cadence of episodes, who's on the podcast, where you advertise the podcast, and how long episodes are.

Interestingly, in a recent BBC news article entitled, 'Is the 'have-a-go' podcaster era coming to an end? In 2023, there are more podcasts out there than ever before, from comedy to news, sport to true crime.

A survey carried out by YouGov suggests that podcasts present one of the biggest growth opportunities for UK media in 2023, with global revenue in the music, radio and podcast market projected to reach $108.3bn (£87.09bn) before the end of 2024.

But despite a decline in podcast longevity, listening figures are still on the rise.

According to a study conducted by Vodafone (late April 2022), the coronavirus pandemic was influential in causing a rise in the consumption of podcasts in the UK, with as many as 42% of respondents saying they listen to podcasts more now than before. This research was conducted in the UK, and it revealed that 69% of respondents said they listened to podcasts at least once or twice a week.

Interestingly, with continued levels of financial growth in the industry, the production of new podcasts has faltered. Of the total number of shows globally, less than a quarter have more than 10 episodes.

When the author first started podcasting in 2004, he remembers everyone asking what an Earth podcasting was. He describes how metaphorically the swimming pool had plenty of space to swim. Now the lanes are crowded, and everyone wants to share their thoughts through such channels. Even coding the required podcast Real Simple Syndication (RSS) feeds has become simplified through online 'push button' technology available from companies such as Anchor (now formally acquired and integrated into Spotify in 2023).

Adding a podcast element to your online strategy can be supportive but not just because your competitor is publishing one. The real value comes from how much it supports your brand and products, subtly and if one can, with an element of fun!

Podcasting can be an effective way to build brand awareness, establish thought leadership, and engage with your audience in a more intimate and conversational way. By creating a podcast that shares insights, tips, and stories related to your industry or niche, you can position yourself as an authority in your field and build trust with your audience.

Moreover, a podcast can also support your products and services by providing a platform to showcase their unique features and benefits. For example, if you sell software, you can create a podcast that demonstrates how to use the software in real-world scenarios or interviews customers who have had success with the product. By doing so, you can educate your audience on the value of your product and increase the likelihood of conversion.

Coming back to the fun aspect of podcasting. By adding an element of fun and personality to your podcast it can help differentiate it from other podcasts in your industry and create a more enjoyable listening experience and improved probability of loyalty from your audience.

Video Content Marketing

Video content can be shared on social media platforms, landing pages, or on a co-marketer's website.

Video content marketing is becoming increasingly important for content strategy roadmaps. With the rise of social media and the popularity of platforms like YouTube, Instagram, and TikTok, video has become one of the most effective ways to reach and engage with audiences.

Video content is highly engaging and can capture viewers' attention more effectively than other forms of content. This is because video content can be more visually appealing, and it can convey information in a more memorable and emotional way.

Video content can take many forms, including explainer videos, product demos, interviews, live streams, and more. This versatility makes video content marketing suitable for a wide range of industries and content types.

Video content can be easily distributed across multiple channels and platforms. This makes it an effective way to increase brand awareness and reach new audiences.

Video content can also help to improve your website's search engine rankings. By optimising your video content with relevant keywords and metadata, you can increase your chances of ranking higher in search results.

However, it is important to note that creating high-quality video content can be time-consuming and expensive. As such, it is important to carefully consider your goals and resources before investing in video content marketing. It is important to carefully consider your goals and resources before investing in video content marketing.

Paid Ad Content Marketing

Paid ads can help you reach a broad audience and allow you to position yourself in all the places you want to be seen — paid ads are especially beneficial when paired with inbound marketing. There are many places you can share paid ads including on social media, landing pages, banners, and sponsored content.

Effective Steps for Content Marketing strategists:

Set measurable goals, for example to - improve brand awareness, boost sales, encourage brand loyalty, increase customer engagement, and build a dialogue with potential/new and existing customers.

Build your Dashboard - As previously outlined, consider key performance indicators that are easier to initially understand and then further develop with confidence.

Decide on the type of content that you will create - consider the audience in terms of customer personas. Lise needs, challenges, product qualities that you offer, success criteria from the customers perspective and potential time availability.

Budgeting and Tools to assist. Plan for the potential to purchase any software or technology to create the content (such as graphic design software like Adobe Photoshop, a subscription to Canva, a camera to take high-quality photos and videos)? Will you need to hire any content marketers or designers (such as artists, writers, editors, designers)? How much will you allocate in terms of funds for advertising space?

Select content channels - For example, Web, social media, Virtual reality/immersive or a mix of virtual and in-person events.

Schedule content and measure effectiveness - Include frequency of content issuing. We recommend a content calendar and tracking all asset metadata. In addition, link back to your dashboard to become better informed of what content is performing, resonating or needs abandonment / archiving, repurposing, or replacing. Content can also be seasonal and subject to fashion trends!

Best Practice Content Calendar Planning for your brand / product

A content calendar is a tool used to plan and organise the content you will create and share across various channels, such as social media, blog posts, email marketing, or any other digital platform. It is a strategic document that helps you to stay organised, maintain consistency, and achieve your marketing goals.

To best use a content calendar to promote your brand and products, follow these steps:

Define your goals:

Before you start creating content, you need to determine your marketing goals. What are you trying to achieve? Is it brand awareness, lead generation, or increasing sales? Once you have your goals in place, you can plan your content to align with them.

Identify your target audience:

Who is your target audience, and what type of content do they prefer? You need to understand their needs, interests, and pain points to create content that resonates with them.

Plan your content:

Use your content calendar to plan your content in advance. This will help you to stay organised, ensure that you have a variety of content types, and that your content is timely and relevant.

Create high-quality content:

Your content needs to be high-quality and engaging to capture your audience's attention. Use visuals, videos, and other multimedia to make your content more interesting.

Schedule your content:

Once you have created your content, you need to schedule it to be shared across various channels. Use your content calendar to plan when and where you will post your content to ensure maximum exposure.

Track your results:

Monitor your content's performance using analytics tools to determine what works best. Use this information to optimise your content calendar and improve your marketing strategy.

By using a content calendar, you can plan and organise your content effectively, increase your brand awareness, engage with your target audience, and ultimately drive more sales for your business.

Let us now look at a content calendar to identify key meta data that refers to assets, characters or storytelling techniques that should not be overused in your content. The approach is similar to what has been previously discussed but we need to identify key content attributes first.

Here are some suggested steps:

Identify the meta data that should not be overused:
Begin by identifying the metadata that you want to monitor. This could be a particular character or group of characters, a specific asset or icon, or a storytelling technique that you feel should not be overused in your content.

Create a system for tracking the meta data:
Next, you will need to create a system for tracking the metadata in your content calendar. This could involve adding a column to your calendar that lists the meta data you want to track, or using colour coding to indicate when certain meta data is used. Many organisations use simple spreadsheets to track the use of assets or consistency or colours or placement of other brands. Think about the number of times you've seen a TV show and a clear positioning of certain, 'trendy' gadgets. The danger is that the use of these 'assets' can date the content making it not evergreen!

Monitor your content:
As you create and post content, monitor how often you use the metadata you are tracking. Record the frequency and location of each instance in your content calendar.

Analyse your data:
After monitoring your content for a set period, analyse your data to determine if the meta data is being overused. Look for patterns or trends that indicate overuse, such as the same character appearing in multiple pieces of content in a short period.

Adjust your content plan:

Based on your analysis, adjust your content plan to reduce the overuse of the identified meta data. This could involve introducing new characters or assets, or exploring different storytelling techniques.

By using a content calendar to track and monitor metadata that should not be overused in your content, you can ensure that your content remains fresh and engaging

Further Benefits of establishing a customer account service:

Convenience:

Customers can access their account information at any time and from any location with an internet connection.

24/7 access:

Online accounts provide customers with the ability to view their account information at any time of the day or night.

Improved customer service:

Online accounts give customers the ability to access their information and manage their accounts without needing to contact customer service.

Faster service:

Customers can quickly update their account information or make changes to their subscription plans without having to wait for a customer service representative to help them.

Personalised experience:

Customers can customise their online account settings and preferences to meet their unique needs.

Security:

Online accounts are password-protected and encrypted, ensuring that customer data is secure and protected from unauthorised access.

Access to billing and payment history:

Customers can view their billing and payment history online, making it easier to keep track of their account activity.

Automatic payments:

Many online accounts allow customers to set up automatic payments, eliminating the need to manually make payments each month.

Easy bill management:

Customers can view and manage their bills online, making it easier to keep track of due dates and payment amounts.

Automatic email notifications:

Customers can receive email notifications when bills are due or when there are changes to their accounts.

Faster communication:

Customers can communicate with customer service representatives online, which can be faster than communicating over the phone.

Easy account updates:

Customers can update their account information online, such as their address, phone number, or email address.

Easy order tracking:

Customers can track their orders online, making it easier to see when their products will arrive.

Access to purchase history:

Customers can view their purchase history online, making it easier to keep track of past orders and purchases.

Faster refunds and returns:

Customers can initiate returns and refunds online, which can be faster and more convenient than returning products in person.

Loyalty rewards:

Many online accounts offer loyalty rewards programs that reward customers for their purchases. In addition, invitation to special events (location dependant and if shared by the customer).

Product recommendations:

Online accounts can provide customers with personalised product recommendations based on their purchase history.

Discounts and promotions:

Customers can receive discounts and promotions through their online accounts.

Access to product manuals:

Customers can access product manuals and other support materials through their online accounts.

Easy warranty registration:

Customers can register their products for warranties online, making the process faster and more convenient.

Product registration tracking:

Customers can track their product registrations and warranties online.

Access to customer reviews:

Customers can read and leave product reviews on the website, providing valuable feedback for other customers.

Personalized content:

Online accounts can provide customers with personalised content based on their interests and purchase history.

Exclusive content:

Customers can access exclusive content, such as webinars, tutorials, and videos, through their online accounts.

Social media integration:

Online accounts can be integrated with social media, making it easier for customers to share their experiences and feedback with others.

Access to customer support resources:

Customers can access customer support resources, such as FAQs and troubleshooting guides, through their online accounts.

Improved communication:

Customers can communicate with other customers through online forums and message boards.

Improved product feedback:

Online accounts can provide customers with a platform to provide feedback on products and services, which can help companies improve their offerings.

Improved company reputation:

Online accounts can help companies build a positive reputation by providing a convenient, personalized, and secure experience for their customers.

Improved customer retention:

Online accounts can help companies retain customers by providing a convenient and personalized experience.

Reduced costs:

Online accounts can help companies reduce costs associated with customer service and billing.

Increased revenue:

Online accounts can help companies increase

5- CONTENT MATURITY MODELS

A Content Maturity Model is a framework that helps you assess and improve your content marketing efforts. Another way to consider these models is in the context of a roadmap for organisations to develop and improve their content marketing capabilities over time. These models typically outline a series of stages or levels that organisations can progress through, each with its own set of benchmarks and best practices. They can also improve resource allocation via understanding what areas of content marketing require the most attention, and where to focus resources for maximum impact.

Content maturity models also help organisations to refine their strategy and tactics to stay ahead of the competition. There are several Content Maturity models utilised by many organisations.

A selection of popular Enterprise Content Marketing Maturity Models:

Content Marketing Institute's Content Marketing Maturity Model:

This model outlines five stages of maturity, starting with "Initial" and progressing to "Mature." The model focuses on areas such as strategy, audience development, content creation, and measurement.

Sirius Decisions' Content Strategy and Operations Maturity Model:

Outlines five stages of maturity, starting with "Unaligned" and progressing to "Optimised." The model focuses on areas such as planning, production, distribution, and measurement.

Aberdeen Group's Content Marketing Maturity Model:

Outlines four stages of maturity, starting with "Novice" and progressing to "Leader." The model focuses on areas such as content development, distribution, measurement, and alignment with sales and marketing goals.

Altimeter's Content Marketing Maturity Model:

Outlines six stages of maturity, starting with "Planning" and progressing to "Governance." The model focuses on areas such as content planning, creation, distribution, measurement, and governance.

Gartner's Content Marketing Maturity Model:

Outlines four stages of maturity, starting with "Unstructured" and progressing to "Optimised." The model focuses on areas such as strategy, planning, creation, distribution, and measurement.

These are just a few examples of Content Maturity Models that organisations can use to guide their content marketing efforts. Each model has its own unique approach, but they all share the goal of helping organisations improve their content marketing capabilities over time.

Dr Savi's ASPECT - Adapting Enterprise Content Maturity Model

The following model is one that I've developed that can be applied to both internal (Intranet) and external web strategies.

Adaptation:

Content can be refreshed, spring-cleaned and 'fit' under more task-based flows and supported navigation:

Skills:

Existing digital content and communications skills can be applied.

Place aka Channels:

The most appropriate communications channel for a digital content item. Assuring that you define your omnichannel strategy from your mission statement.

Engage with Experts of your content.

On your team to propose and create exemplar content. Obtain content and its ownership from subject matter experts and those that truly know how to compose good messaging.

Assure standards and Content Techniques

That can be demonstrated and socialised effectively.

In summary, models should support a platform, establish publishing standards (include the imparting of knowledge transfer for the development of future standards) and move existing content using online techniques that assure content is on message throughout the life of its purpose.

An Intranet model for Content Refresh Projects

The following stages ensure development and assuring ongoing consistency for content governance:

Assessing:

- Move away from inherited structures & existing /current content:
- Current state assessment & capturing what is good.
- Review external analysis, if third party organisations are invited and report on existing content or historic content.

Piloting:

To prove content change is worthy & can establish standards and experimenting with the, 'art of the possible'.

Structuring:

To scale with good consideration for architectural design and User Experience. Effectively, managing expectations from the outset

Continuity for sustaining investment in change:

Ensuring standards are in place and knowledge transfer to facilitate confidence for department-based content managers/owners. Assuring content service optimisation

Assuring Progression to verify change:

Validating self-sufficiency & posted content through consistent monitoring of original agreed content objectives and success factors. Verifying Return on content development investment and demonstrating practical innovation

SALE
NEW STYLES ADDED!
UP TO 80% OFF

6 - CREATING CUSTOMER VALUED CONTENT

At its core, the definition of content is published information in the context of developing online images and text or anything your company creates for typically your website or application that is well executed, relevant and engages your visitors. Even better, if the same content is also search engine optimised (SEO) then your business is way ahead of the pack! Increasingly, a more recent development is the science of Content Marketing.

This term can be understood as: Consistency, i.e: Regular posting of content Customer-centric, i.e: Relevant published and sign-posted content Collaborative, i.e: Working with your internal teams to find key knowledge nuggets that will be resonant with your both your brand and your customers.

Potentially, content marketing is marketing designed to heighten the potential of your customers' preferred brands. Then, any anticipated campaign being planned must also include an understanding and provision for the impact it will have on your approach, method, and content idea selection process.

Content Purpose

The main consideration for any content must be its purpose. It's important to consider if the content being published will enhance your company's presence in the market? If so, what is the end outcome expected? Is it more sales, more visitors or simply getting customers to stay on your website, to encourage browsing and eventually be influenced to make a purchase.

Imagine you're in a shop and your eye catches something other than what your original intent was. In effect you've been attracted to something that resonates with you. I'm sure you'll agree with a situation where you've gone into a physical (aka outside of your virtual world) shop or bought something and either left with your target item and even more items! Or sometimes something completely different! Sadly, you may have forgotten what you originally went in for and walked away with nothing but being confused or overwhelmed. Potentially, the same works for browsing on a retailer's website. What can you place strategically to attract and maintain interest?

We're now beginning to border into the territory of screen design, the effective use of screen estate and layout - also known as the science behind effective user experiences. Often referred to or known as 'UX' for short, there are many books on this subject. One of the pioneers of this type of thinking is Jessie James Garrett. His diagram titled, 'The Elements of User Experience' launched his popularity in the mainstream web design community in early 2000. It was later published as a book. In a 2005 paper, Garrett coined the term 'Ajax' to describe the asynchronous technology behind emerging services like Google Maps, as well as the resulting user experience which made it possible to browse without interruption by eliminating the reloading of an entire web page.

Content Relevance

Understanding what your customer will be interested in is the first place to start in terms of defining relevance.

Relevance has two lenses, the reader aka recipient, and the originator, i.e: the composer that has the original intent. One technique is to list potential content topics and add to each one an aspect of 'Ascension'. The definition of Ascension is the act or process of moving or rising especially to a higher or more powerful position.

Content Ascension is about considering what next steps would be ideal after your content has been consumed. Typically, what journey would you like them to pursue and how can they be led in what should be a non-subversive, genuine path to become a customer - enticing them along a route for them to want to purchase and to come back again and again.

Interestingly, many systems are available online today that, 'plant' identifiers and trackers to orchestrate journeys. In addition, artificial intelligence (AI) can also be implemented to change what content is presented - if a customer is repeatedly viewing a product but has not decided to commit to a purchase.

For example, a customer may be viewing a particular car model and colour. If he/she has viewed the same item several times in the same week one suggestion or conclusion is that they're quite keen. AI can test and create alternative customer journey pathways. Much of this technology assumes that some tracking has been accepted or consented to by the customer on entry to the associated website.

Fashion related content

It's fascinating to note complementary fashion content in the form of experiential video/ Blogs. Today, fashion-based topics include discussing mood wear, perfecting accessories, the concept of sustainability, organising your wardrobe and observing influencers. Another approach is to introduce the element of fun and practical tips. Such content hinges on the need for investing in super visuals & storytelling techniques!

Earning customer engagement

Typical steps to earn customer engagement include Being relevant, concise, clear about intent/ objective and making content easily digestible. Often, poor supportive content, e.g: Poor thought out FAQs can result in a lack of loyalty. Basic interactions such as order returns need to use well-structured layouts to easily locate information and reduce complexity in customer required actions and in turn be supported via associated responsive company procedures. It's all very well bringing in customers with great content, it's essential that service content is action oriented, supporting accountability and rapid issue resolution.

The value of implementing a Customer Account

Having a customer account can be a valuable component of a mature content management system (discussed earlier), as it allows for personalised content delivery and tracking of customer behaviour and preferences. Other factors include content creation management processes, governance structures, and technology infrastructure. Ultimately, your chosen content management maturity model should reflect both the unique needs and goals of the organisation and its customers. Encouraging a customer account for both an existing and new customer can facilitate loyalty through exclusive offers and content. For example, consider a car manufacturer or car dealer. New models and exclusive open day invitations could be issued with access to associated areas of a firm's website.

Impart the importance of a differentiated digital storefront.

According to Fortune Magazine a survey conducted in 2022 suggested that up to 82% of shopping carts are abandoned before checkout. Additionally, 50.5% in large online consumer marketplaces would like to see more content on the items they are about to purchase before they commit. Small Biz Genius outlines that 61% of customers abandon a purchase due to a lack of trust in the platform and its brand. In addition, researchers confirm that 85% of customers like to research the products they are about to purchase online through content marketing. These observations suggest that content that expands the value proposition of products can ensure that visitors can become customers and that customers will become brand advocates of the platform itself.

Content is King

This phrase shown above originated in 1996. However, if content is King / Queen, then content writers should be deemed as warriors! Back then the Internet was still in its infancy. Interestingly, Microsoft CEO Bill Gates had the foresight to recognise the cultural impact that content would have in the not-so-distant future. However, the challenge today is to weave words together in such a manner that they strike the right chord in the minds of an intended audience whilst maintaining the identity of a company brand. In summary, content is now more about context and our customers are now the King / Queen!

Regardless of age, shoppers now expect a robust array of content when they shop online. This includes 5-8 images, 2-5 videos and even an average of 8-13 questions to be answered by the brand itself. If consumers don't see what they are looking for, they often leave the associated product page outright. In fact, according to a recent Salsify research report, nearly 70% of consumers chose a lack of product information as a reason they've left an online retail site. This even exceeded the number of shoppers that used a high price tag as a deal breaker. Authentic and accurate content is key, considered in the context of communicating trusted product experience aka getting the balance right between a product image and supporting information. Engaging stories often fuel one's intrigue to stay longer and eventually buy!

Social media Content

Social media channels have recently introduced features allowing retailers to upload their product catalogues to ease discovery. Notably, Instagram has integrated checkout experiences to streamline conversion. This has driven a clear shift in social commerce purchases.

According to Civic Science in 2022, the percentage of US adults who have purchased products directly on social media has nearly doubled over the past few years—from 13% in Q4 2018 to 25% in Q3 2020. Much of this activity resides on social media platforms currently, but where it goes next may be even more interesting.

The Era of all things Digital

Recent research from Deloitte suggests that "In the era of all things digital, consumers have higher expectations: they want their interactions with businesses and the products and services they buy from them to be personalised."

Furthermore, Michael Porter's competitive forces model suggests that developing high switching costs for competitors aka making it harder for competitors to enter your market. This approach also applies to keeping customers, for example via making the customer experience great with beautifully presented and unique products, timely delivery & super customer service. Investment in unique customer centric omni-channel based content marketing and supportive lifestyle interaction is key.

Investing in Content Technology enablers

Recent published statistics from researchers at CONTENTSTACK in 2021 suggested that: 33% of marketing budgets go towards technology, with 28% of that total budget going to infrastructures such as Content Management Systems. 92% of companies face challenges in translating content into different languages. Only 29% of companies integrate their Content Management System (CMS) with a translation management system or language service provider. One of the most interesting reveals is that 91% of customers want to pick up from where they left off when they contact a customer service representative, no matter what channel they use, for example, moving from a bot to a 'real' person.

Journey Orchestration

Journey Orchestration is a service built on a particular content management system that allows tailored individual journeys for every customer based on their previous behaviour and preferences. Once in place, an online retail company can anticipate individual needs through real-time insight. It is also possible to configure and use an event to trigger an individual journey. However, investment in consent, tracking, building, and maintaining technical infrastructure will also be needed to realise any benefits - together with interpretation of emerging patterns and re-testing if the same impact results under varying scenarios. (Read more by researching on example products that conduct online tagging and associated storage repositories, for example: Treasure Data and Thunderhead).

The importance of Visual based content

Recent research (2021) suggests 62% of generation Z (Gen Z) and millennial consumers are keen on visual search. In addition, over 80% of Gen Z respondents suggest that the look of a retailer's website impacts their purchasing decisions. However, images must be supported by accompanying narrative or a call to action, especially for online consumer opportunities.

An interesting developing area is timeless fashion and style. This impacts not only classic clothes but new styles and trends. The same principles apply to interior design. A cool way to consider this trend is to combine elevated basics, sophisticated centrepieces and streamlined outfits that avoid being identified by a particular fashion trend or fashion decade. Fashion is cyclical in nature and 'mix and match' continues to be a favourite activity amongst consumers.

7
8
14
15

7 - INSPIRING CONTENT SAYINGS

Enjoy the following saying to help motivate you to become super content strategists. **Be inspired:**

'Without strategy, content is just stuff, and the world has enough stuff' - Arjan Basu

'The Joy of dressing is an Art'- John Galliano

Your goal should be to own quality time in your customer's inbox.'- Andrew Davis

'70% of consumers say plentiful product page details are critical to their shopping.' - Salsify

'Content is King'- Bill Gates (1996)

'Data is a Tool for enhancing intuition' - Hillary Mason

'Media and commerce will converge as checkout attaches to shoppable content'- Insider Intelligence Magazine 2022

'70% of consumers say plentiful product page details are critical to their shopping.' - Salsify

'Content builds relationships. Relationships are built on trust. Trust drives revenue'- Andrew Davis

'Your website is the window of your business. Keep it fresh, keep it exciting.'- Jay Conrad Levison

'The key ingredient to better content is separating the single from the stream.' - David Hahn

'People remember 80% of what they see & 20% of what they read'- ViSenze

'I don't design clothes, I design dreams'- Ralph Lauren

'All of your customers are partners in your mission.' - Shep Hyken

Closing words for our Primer.

As you come to the end of this book, you should now have a solid understanding of content marketing strategies and how to implement them effectively. You have learned how to create high-quality content, engage with your audience, and drive traffic to your website. All these skills will equip you to develop an effective Content strategy roadmap.

The aim of this book was to give you a good primer aka foundation in what it takes to build effective content marketing and management strategies.

It's important to remember that content marketing is not a one-time event but an ongoing process that requires consistent effort and continuous improvement. Keep analysing your results and fine-tuning your strategies to stay ahead of the competition.

In today's digital age, content marketing has become a crucial aspect of every business's marketing strategy. By creating valuable content that resonates with your audience, you can build brand awareness, establish credibility, and drive leads and sales.

So, as you embark on your content marketing journey, remember to stay focused, stay creative, and stay true to your brand's message. With the right strategies in place, you can achieve great success and take your business to new heights.

Open process
Community
Strong Design Skills

8 - EPILOGUE

It's easy to skim past advertisements online, if you're on a free service, for example, YouTube. You simply don't wait for the full advertisement to finish and watch the on-screen minimum countdown seconds display before you swipe/brush them away. However, increasingly you're 'forced' to watch or listen to the entire pitch! Do we skip the advertisements because they're irrelevant? Or are we too impatient to reach and digest the content we originally searched for? This issue presents a challenge for online advertisers and content designers that support the selling of products. Advertisers are now having to resort to more elaborate adverts.

The flip side of the latter is when you're interested in a product. In that case, one is often keen to watch and capture every piece of product related content available, from images at every angle, technical specifications, experiential video reviews from experts to everyday peer-based consumers. Sadly, in the case of sites like TripAdvisor, typically a hotel review can have lots of positive reviews, but we often focus on a few of the bad ones! The latter is of course out of our control.

Ensuring your content is authentic and genuine will be key for future marketeers. This is because consumers are increasingly becoming more discerning about the content they consume and are looking for genuine and trustworthy content from brands.

In the age of social media, where anyone can create and publish content, consumers have become more sceptical of marketing messages that feel overly promotional. As a result, brands that focus on creating authentic and genuine content are likely to gain more trust and loyalty from their customers.

In addition to authenticity and genuineness, future marketers may also need to focus on creating personalised content that resonates with their target audience. With the proliferation of data and technology, marketers have access to a wealth of information about their customers' preferences, behaviours, and interests. By leveraging this data, marketers can create tailored content that speaks directly to their customers' needs and interests.

Another important consideration for future marketers is the need to create content that is optimised for different platforms and devices. With the rise of mobile and voice-based search, marketers need to ensure that their content is easily accessible and digestible on different devices and platforms.

Who will really be writing content in the future?

In the early 1990s many websites were built on HTML and didn't have mature safety markers and consumer security policies. Much has changed but one area that has been a constant is the ability to tell stories. Certainly, graphics have changed, and one could argue with more virtual reality headsets emerging, there will need to be another revolution in terms of how sales propositions are pitched together with adherence to brand consistency.

With the increasing abilities of Artificial Intelligence (AI) to create content from scraping the web, there is now a new urgency to be authentic, original and 'human'. I'm confident that the human spirit will ensure that we adapt to changing conditions. The basic principles of age-old story telling will no doubt be challenged and will need to morph.

For help with developing your online web strategy, consultancy services are available via: www.savileaders.com

9 - ABOUT THE AUTHOR

Dr Savi Arora

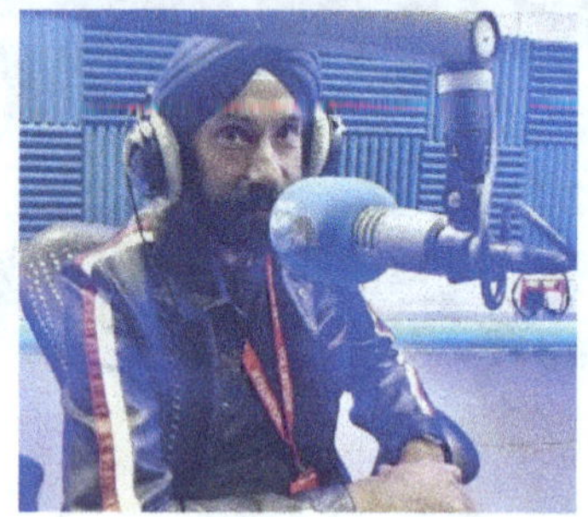

Dr Savi is a renowned web strategist & accomplished Programme Director. He's written several books and articles on best practice in areas such as Project Management and Creative Techniques. With over 40 years of experience as a company programme Director working at National Semiconductor Corp, Computacenter, Vodafone, O2, Microsoft, GSK, 3 mobile, SkyTV, Next PLC and Honda he has a host of real-world experiences to share. In addition, supportive academic credentials: A Postgraduate in Management, MBA, and PhD.

Dr Savi has worked on Sky.com/shop, O2 Priority Moments, NHS national eLearning rollout, the first apps via 3, My Vodafone App and Honda Marine, just to mention a few. His approach has always been to build on measured phased implementations with an understanding of analytics, business continuity and longevity from the outset. He believes in realising success for all that he works with.

Further Reading:

"Content Marketing for Dummies" by Susan Gunelius
"Epic Content Marketing" by Joe Pulizzi
"Content Strategy for the Web" by Kristina Halvorson and Melissa Rach
"The Content Code" by Mark W. Schaefer
"Everybody Writes" by Ann Handley
"The New Rules of Marketing and PR" by David Meerman Scott
"Content Rules" by Ann Handley and C.C. Chapman
"Youtility" by Jay Baer
"Contagious" by Jonah Berger
"The Art of SEO" by Eric Enge, Stephan Spencer, Jessie Stricchiola
"SEO for Growth" by John Jantsch and Phil Singleton
"Search Engine Marketing, Inc." by Mike Moran and Bill Hunt
"The Content Strategy Toolkit" by Meghan Casey
"Master Content Marketing" by Pamela Wilson
"The Content Strategy At Work" by Margot Bloomstein
"Content Marketing Works" by Arnie Kuenn
"The Ultimate Guide to Content Marketing & Digital PR" by David Meerman Scott
"Digital Marketing Handbook" by Sarvesh Shrivastava
"The Content Marketing Coach" by Bradley Gunnery
"The Content Marketing Handbook" by Robert W. Bly
"The Content Marketing Revolution" by Mark Masters
"Marketing 4.0" by Philip Kotler, Hermawan Kartajaya, and Iwan Setiawan
"Killing Marketing" by Joe Pulizzi and Robert Rose
"The One Hour Content Plan" by Meera Kothand
"Content Inc." by Joe Pulizzi
"The Power of Visual Storytelling" by Ekaterina Walter and Jessica Gioglio

"The Big Book of Content Marketing" by Andreas Ramos and Stephanie Diamond

"The Psychology of Marketing" by Pauline J. Sheldon and Juliette Koning

"Content Marketing Made Easy" by Tommy Mello

"The Art of Content Marketing" by Kevin M. Ryan and Pamela J. Vaughn

"Inbound Marketing" by Brian Halligan and Dharmesh Shah

"The Content Trap" by Bharat Anand

"The Copywriter's Handbook" by Robert W. Bly

"Contagious Content" by Susan Gunelius

"The Business of Expertise" by David C. Baker

"Building a StoryBrand" by Donald Miller

"Hug Your Haters" by Jay Baer

"The Adweek Copywriting Handbook" by Joseph Sugarman

"The Storytelling Edge" by Joe Lazauskas and Shane Snow

"Content Marketing Secrets" by Marc Guberti

"The Social Media Bible" by Lon Safko

"Content Marketing Playbook" by Jason Miller

"How Brands Become Icons" by Douglas B. Holt

"The Marketing Book" by Jason McDonald

"They Ask You Answer" by Marcus Sheridan

www.ingramcontent.com/pod-product-compliance
Lightning Source LLC
Chambersburg PA
CBHW072151230526
45467CB00042B/1665

* 9 7 9 8 3 9 2 6 5 6 7 1 4 *